SHAPES, SHADES AND FACES

Moferefere
Lekorotsoana

African Perspectives Publishing
PO Box 95342, Grant Park 2051, South Africa
www.africanperspectives.co.za

© Moferefere Lekorotsoana January 2018

ISBN PRINT 978-0-6399187-1-6
ISBN DIGITAL 978-0-6399187-0-9

Typesetting and cover by Gail Day
Cover image by Henrik Sorensen

Contents

Preface

From the onset, my interest in poetry came from my fascination with how words could express and, at the same time, carry the accumulation of our experience(s). The experience could be simple or complex, sad or joyful, despairing or hopeful. It is about how the word(s) looks into me or the other, see in one's recess, and express the moment without being held back.

My journey to publish began with some trepidation. I was anxious about being vulnerable, cautious of being revealed and revealing about those I have known. Consequently, my initial inclination was that this is a deeply private and personal thing I should reserve to myself. Otherwise, only my children would, later, access these readings as a means of catching a glimpse into my life, the people with who I broke bread, the places I walked and the times I lived in. Yet this whole experience, as it was the case in its private undertaking, was cathartic and one of the memory of where it came from.

My inspiration for writing, and poetry in particular, is my father – Ntate Maitse Lorenti Lekorotsoana. He wrote for *Moeletsi oa Basotho* – a Mazenod Press weekly, published in Roma – Lesotho, a of copy of which was avidly read in my home. Significantly, though, I was drawn to how he used words to describe events and living. His poetry, often in esoterica inked in beautiful lithograph, left me spellbound. I suppose his writings substituted for the fact that he never spoke much.

Related to my father too, something else that had a profound impact on my poetry was his eloquence and brilliance in Sesotho recital – more like today's spoken word and freestyle. Together with our next door neighbour, Ntate Langman Mokhoabane, they would get into spontaneous jibes to test the other's prowess in this art form. Almost endless banters – characterised by postures and strides at intimidating the opponent – would ensue either at the crack of dawn, prior to work as the township prepared to rise, or at dusk as the township settled down after supper. The two old men would revel us with historical tales, their workplace struggles, resistance, sorrow and enchantment, accounts of life in the township, etc. They were amazing. It's as if I can hear and see them now; hence the smile on my face.

These experiences left an indelible mark on me. Much, much earlier on, when I started out writing, I did so in Sesotho. I so wished to emulate them but, unfortunately, I couldn't sustain it except a few remaining writings and some I do now and then. I couldn't match them and their Sesotho but, at least, English offered a sanctuary.

My endeavour with English was encouraged greatly by Ausi 'Nana – better known as Ma'am Maki to the younger ones, and Mistress Moorosi to the older generation. She was my Sesotho and English teacher at different times in my Bantu education schooling. Somehow, she insisted that I write, even enquiring when I had or had not written. So the courage and confidence grew with each day, to the point I would surprise her with an offering.

I believe bo-Ntate Maitse le Mokhoabane le ausi 'Nana are watching now, ba bona mesebetsi ea liatla tsa bona *ka phaka tsa mabitla*.

A constant pillar is my sister, 'Me Mokgampepe Mary-Dolores Lekorotsoana Zumo. Throughout, ever since I can remember, her voice kept on saying, "*hey oena, o ntse o ngola tje?!*", and later it was, "*o phatlalatsa neng?*". When you have that constant voice – your older sister nogal ...

Wondering through living I came across this fellow, a wonderful friend and comrade, Siven Maslamoney. After fortuitously bumping into one of my writings – a short story, he never let go nudging and encouraging me to write more and publish.

One afternoon, thanks to the late Arabi Mocheke – a fabulous soul, friend and comrade – I landed with a sumptuous plate of samp on Rose Francis' stoep; where the story of friendship and conversations about writings were reignited. "Don't you want to publish?", I don't even remember how we got there but the next thing she was sitting with my collection of poetry and short stories. At first she was comfortable with my anxieties about publishing. But, clearly it was a ruse. Roughly about three or so years ago we were back to the first question. It turned out I was at ease this time.

My journey for words to express and carry the accumulation of my personal and our collective experiences would be incomplete without the imitable, ever-present, larger than life, Rre Professor Keorapetse William Kgositsile – our national poet laureate. He shouldered our insignificant and, sometimes perilous, life in word for moons on end. We are fortunate, those of us who share bread and word with him; we who he chooses to call his comrades, we he graciously helps and to who he conveys his immense knowledge and experience. I still recall him say at the beginning of this project when I made the request — at the suggestion of bro Mandla Langa; "*don't you think because you are my comrade I will let you off easy.*" And, by God, he was so true to his word.

With gratitude to the living dead and the living, the words that began in the small town of Maletsoai, Aliwal North, on the banks of the Senqu; words which have meandered through the streets of many a township and city — here and abroad, running and strolling; have finally found their way in this collection. They are a memory and a celebration of living, love, laughter and tears. Reminiscent of the old men who spoke the word and left an imprint on me.

To my children, Neo and Jako Lekorotsoana, may these words help express and carry the accumulation of your live's experiences.

As a celebration of living, love, laughter and tears; they come in their *shapes, shades and faces*.

To you, one and all, Motaung enoa oa Hlalele o a leboha hle.

Introduction

In the introduction to Sterling Plumpp's STEPS TO
BREAK THE CIRCLE (Third World Press, Chicago, 1974),
which deals with some of the confused and confusing
aspects of some of the tendencies in the 1960s in
North America, I point out to the proliferation of
garbage that passed for Black poetry. "Much of the
ranting," I observed, "was no more than a bunch of
slogans with ready sentimental appeal, headed for the
marketplace."

A little later, we here in Mzansi, with our mimetic
tendencies, were subjected to a similar kind of ranting
and, as our lack of luck would be, this torture lasted for
a longer period. In fact, it is not over yet.

But the poet worth the label, deals with what it is to
be alive. As Gwendolyn Brooks put it,

"Art is life worked with; is life
wheedled, or whelmed:
assessed:
clandestine, but evoked."

The point of departure of the poet's imagination,
unless the supposed poet be no more than a word
juggler playing perverse games, is always life.

As long as I have known Moferefere Lekorotsoana
and have worked closely with him for the past six years
now, I have never heard him refer to himself as a poet.
But his SHAPES SHADES AND FACES is a remarkable
proverbial breath of fresh air. His vision is not blurred;
it is focused, controlled and illumines the textures of
whatever shapes, shades and faces he looks at and
into and responds to. No syrupy-sweet, nauseating
embellishments which some, with delusions of being

poets, mistake for expressive language. Lekorotsoana carves his poems out of clear, simple, lean, supple and precise prose.

The first section of this collection is titled *Inner Voices*. It is divided into six *movements* which begin with the perceived anguish suffered when a sense of aloneness, a lack of belonging, is so intense a self-destructive cynicism sets in:

> I shall not think
> not feel
> I shall love to hate
> and hate to love

By the end of the *second movement* a fear of interacting with others has firmly set in:

> I shall remain indifferent
> for if I do not
> I might end up foolish
> I think I might feel
> I might love

However, since this morbid, death-bound nonsense can neither be desirable nor sustained, by the *third movement* it is jettisoned:

> all days are new
> all days change
> and bring changes
> today you mourn and cry
> tomorrow you laugh and dance

And by the end of the *sixth movement*, the final one, there is hope and determination:

> ... to know how to think
> to feel
> to love
> to celebrate life

From this point Lekorotsoana takes the reader on an exploration to where he has been. And he has been to many places, both literally and figuratively. When he waxes philosophical he pushes, perhaps I should say persuades, the reader to consider and confront certain aspects of life s/he might otherwise never have bothered to look at, as in *Mortality*:

> in the meaningful-meaninglessness
> of the end of life
> we grapple with its purpose
> when young lives commit suicide
> we beg for higher knowledge
> but we find no answer
> then we are thrown into utter despair
> because we wish they spoke
> we wish they confided in us

His explorations continue unabated like any struggle, with determined resolve. He looks into history and the ancestral ties that bind us, the past that cannot be forgotten lest we lose the sense of who we are. There is also collective amnesia. There are departures and returns, exile and longing, solidarity, hope and hopelessness, war, love, hate, greed, death, love and love-making, loneliness as distinct from aloneness, landscapes evoked, betrayal, and much more in the course of human action and interaction.

Finally, whatever he chooses to explore, to look at and into, whether actual or imagined, he manages to make real.

Keorapetse Kgositsile
National Poet Laureate

SHAPES, SHADES AND FACES

Moferefere
Lekorotsoana

Inner voices

first movement

I shall not think
not feel
I shall love to hate
and hate to love
maybe I shall love no more
and be indifferent to the world
I shall take nothing seriously
all seriousness I will shun
I shall make life easy for me

I shall accept people as they are
what they are
from where they are
I shall take their pace in life
not rush them
not slow them

I shall not underestimate anything anymore
I shall not work with some people
for I might take them seriously
I might think about them
I might love them
if I work with them I shall be indifferent
not think about them
not feel towards them
not love them
for love is painful
and loving is foolish.

second movement

when you take the world seriously
it makes you feel ridiculous
when you think about people
when you feel towards them
they wonder what is wrong with you
therefore, I shall let everything
and everyone
pass by without notice

I shall not open myself to others
for they are ready to distract me
I shall not get close to them
for their fears block them
from relating to me
yet they expect me to be fearless
I shall look at them as things without potential
without self-confidence,
without readiness to take a risk
I shall not be hopeful about them

I shall give to those who want to be given
I shall receive from those who offer
In all this exchange
I shall remain indifferent
for if I do not
I might end up foolish
I think I might feel
I might love

third movement

all days are new
all days change
and bring changes
today you mourn and cry
tomorrow you laugh and dance

be ready to learn from each day
be willing to hear from the seasons
be open to see from changes
all flow so well
all flow at their pace
at their own time
they have all perfected the skill of patience

henceforth I shall learn to wait
I shall wait
I shall not be hasty
I shall be patient
when I lose control
I shall wait
for things to fall back
into place again

I shall think
I shall not get frustrated
when others cannot think
I shall feel
I shall not feel stupid
when it seems others do not feel
I shall love
even though it is demanding
even though it is a slow process

I shall wait for others
to think, to feel, to love
I shall work towards perfecting this skill
I shall be patient
so that I can know how to wait
I shall wait until I succeed
every day shall be a waiting day
wait for people
wait for every thing

I shall wait
maybe I will understand the days
the seasons
and the changes

fourth movement

it is a whole new world for me
a world to think
a world to feel
a world to love
and all shall be done selflessly
I shall always wait

openness shall characterise my days
I shall not forget to smile
I shall wait
for everything will be done in love
with respect
with thought
with feeling

no longer shall I hate to love
no longer shall I love to hate
I shall love always

the journey before me is long
sometimes it makes me want to give up
sometimes clarity seems elusive

Therefore
in my prayer I shall wait
wait to see God
not an empty concept
God who is not locked
in a tabernacle
wait to see God
who does not play tricks on me
the God who is not imposed on me
the God who is no idol
I shall wait to see God
who transforms and challenges
one who loves that I can love
one who ensures the success of my journey
one who is one with me.

I am tired of
the God of chess games
one who is an absolute king
one who makes me a simple person
an exploitative and manipulative God
one who doesn't give chance
to mistakes and risks
No. I am tired of that God.
I shall wait

fifth movement

I shall not wait
for the sake of waiting
I shall wait
to assess my egocentric attitudes
maybe I love only for my sake
or think simply for myself
or feel for the sake of it

are my relations only for selfish interest?
do I model people in terms of my views only?
do I allow others to be themselves too?
am I afraid lest they discover me?

I shall work hard to change
I shall strive to commit
to those I hold dear
not hurt them
I shall give time and patience
To accompany others
in their journey through life

I shall take risks
in all that I open myself up to
I shall risk hate for love
risk losing myself
losing hold and control on things
I shall risk being destroyed
risk everything

sixth movement

above all I shall hope
and have hope
hope that things will change
that I will love fully
treat others as human
and discover what it means to love
to live
to be human
Hope to have faith
to be built up and grow
I will learn to hope for others
have hope from them
and have hope in them
Hope to know how to think
to feel
to love
to celebrate life

Dying silently

respect this skeleton
adorned in flesh and beautiful robes
passing smiles and wise greetings
like a diplomat from abroad
not touched by the scene around

oh! the agony
of an uncared for soul
the willingness to live persists
the spirit refuses to jet off
it parades around
and all is well

like a patient dying of cancer
life slowly passing away
carefully and quietly
the dark cloud
creeping in
like a tree
carved from within by a worm
pathways immeasurable in size
innumerable in number
daily continuing to die

how can one live this life?
why is the spirit not flying away?
maybe
it wants to crush even the skeleton
taking away every thing
even it-self

maybe it is a lamentation which will go
like the rest
it will come to pass
and like what went with the wind
it will be restored

no one sees
the decomposing insides
noses are immune they can't smell
thickened by the glories of causes
the greatest of glories
respect the dead
especially those who die from within
who die smiling
even in the presence of
the worst of their enemies

maybe
they are not immune
rather
they want to take the stench
and the worms with it
unaware they hijacked
a compost from within

but then they will smell the corpse
in their hands
by then there will be
no taste of glory
because this body shall be
long gone
dead from inside

...We are

in the silence
of hearts and minds
images of those felt dearly
creep into our hiding places
dreaded moments
of silent torture
are the only threads
that connect us
only in them
do we feel
touch and hold

in toughest moments of alone-ness
time grows long
and spaces widen
in times of deepest reflection
and contemplation
being makes sense
living is meaningful
the essence of existence
is realised

no one is alone
even in the silence of our thoughts
alone-ness
is but a figment of the imagination
in the deepest silence
of our being
we are never alone
for even in that singular
we are

Streetwise

all over the city
filthy,
miserable creatures roam
in all shapes and sizes
zonked out of their minds
living in an illusionary-real world

products of a bitter system
a vicious cycle
faeces of the wealthy
pests
an annoyance, an irritant,
bloody beggars, criminals,
scum of the world.

at night back to basics
down by the dark alley
in cardboard boxes
dirty torn blankets
by the fire...
having sex.

at sunrise
like cockroaches in the kitchen
like flies on shit
they infest the streets

nothing to show for their lives
shamefully they die
every day
every season, every...

Ka phaka tsa mabitla[1]

they watch us
motaung[2]
ka phaka tsa mabitla

they continue to live
in us
among us
with us
we are their gifts
in us
they see gifts of themselves
in our becoming
we are gifts
of ourselves to them

we are their mirrors
the embodiment of their spirit
we do not see them
we feel their everlasting presence
as long as we live
they too live
and continue
to watch us

1   *a Sesotho expression suggesting that ancestors watch over us.*
    Literally, they see from the heaps of the graves
2   *tau means lion, which is a totem, and people who use it as a*
    clan name are called Bataung (plural), motaung (singular)

The mountain kingdom

in the land of their birth
see the huge and fearless
mountains
as they move upwards to grab the sky
shaking hands with the gods
powerful and serene are
the plains and the valleys
of the land
as they allow the shepherd
to watch after livestock

see the splendour
of the monstrous and fearsome
gorges
as you walk into them and
never seem to come out
as you enter their ever
wide open mouths
deep through into their bottom-less pits
at times
you think they will close up
and swallow you
and yet
right then
they seem to laugh
at the stranger
that is you

in the dryness of the land
touch the pain
the hardships and sufferings

of its inhabitants
in its greener pastures
its quiet streams
flowing rivers
greet the smiles of its people

this is the land of mountains and hills
of cliffs and rock
of streams and rivers
of huts and late night
cooking fires
the beautiful land of their birth

this is their life
their past, present and future
on this land they are born
on it they eat
on it they grow and are initiated
into manhood and womanhood

on this land
they raise their babies
shed their tears
and share their laughter
the old men playing *morabaraba*[3]
and smoking pipe
at the courtyard
the old women *bending the knee*[4]
shepherds playing sticks

in the open fields
and young women waiting patiently
for fountains to fill
their calabashes

a kingdom in the mountains
where humankind blends with nature
where every gorge, mountain
hill...resounds
when the thunderous bolts
of the heavens
send forth their word
in a gigantic voice

the beautiful land of their birth
where they lived and are buried
yet continue to live
hence we come back
to touch base
dig into the roots
find our origins
sense peace
feel freedom and love

as you leave
they remain
in the land of their birth
their heritage
where the mountains hover over you
to give their blessings
and somehow
you hear a voice
"*khotso, pula, nala*"[5]

---

3   *a game, drawn on the ground using stones – symbolising cattle
    – played by shepherds/boys (similar to Western board games)*
4   *a direct translation of the Sesotho "ho fina lengoele/lengole";
    meaning the brew is the best*
5   *literally; peace, rain, prosperity. A Sesotho expression wishing
    someone well, similar to the English Godspeed*

E batlang baneng?[6]

through their eyes
you can almost tell the pain
young kids coming to a sanctuary
but experience the most
excruciating of hells

through their eyes
you see innocence
but through the same eyes
you can also sense and touch
the gruesome scenes they have seen
the persecution they have endured

through their eyes
you can almost grasp their plea
for help
to you, to God
the God in whose name
they were abused
the God their torturers pray
the one they also
said night prayers to
maybe the night prayer was panacea
to heal the deep wounds
in their frail bodies and souls

through their eyes you see torment
anguish and fear
beyond this hell is emptiness
justice is not just

it sacrifices little children
it favours power and status

through their eyes
we are questioned and criticised
through their eyes
we are accused
charged and found guilty
of complacency
of indifference
of failure to defend the helpless

as their eyes pierce
sharply into you
they send a chill through your bones

can you hear their voices
in the streets
in your homes?
can you see their faces?

you imagine
then see your child
 a pain shoots inside you
turning into a loud cry

6 literally; what has it to do with the children. Figuratively it
   means that no matter what happens, the children must be
   spared or should be never harmed

17

Down, deep in pain

a love poem I want to create
the words are there
but the energy is lost
my hand refuses to hold the pen
I want to speak
but my heart is up to my neck
my throat has run dry

I watch you stride along
alone into the unknown
I cannot accompany you
maybe yours
should be a solitary walk

if I could bring you back
I would joyfully do so
tell you all is well
but that would be a lie

I hurt
pain strikes through my bones
my heart is pierced
it is burdened with grief
nights are lone-some
my pillows are drenched with my sobbing
my eyes are baggy
like those of the aged

to no avail I cry
my sadness of no consequence
what has happened

has happened
and I am left alone
paralysed by a pain
of untold immensity

so go on seeker of stability
move on
once sojourner in my tent
move on to security and comfort
this space
you now leave behind is unstable
with your pleasantries stride along

I remain
lonely and hurt
for my leisure I will write
not romance but tragedy
dirges instead of love poems
and my song
kodi ya malla
pina ya mahlomola[7]

tsela tshweu[8]
my once faithful friend
my once-upon-a-time
companion
no blessing from me
but tears from my heart
for your journey
my pain is unbearable
it does not permit courtesies

7   *a dirge*
8   *farewell/go well, literally meaning white/bright path*

Separation

if only I could forgive
obliterate the anger
and resentment
erase the hatred
I now feel
if only I could hold you tight
feel the warmth
of your passion and want
like once
when I grew hard, and bulged
inside your unimaginable depths
but how can I feel
and forgive
when our once unfathomable
secret union
is now my detachment
something you made known to another?

Nights

these are endless
and sleepless nights
eyes stare into the dark abyss
in conspiracy
a poisoned mind
with unpalatable memories
as the heart bleeds with rage
with time ticking away
like a bomb
soon to explode

I don't want to hurt (anymore)

Part I

I have emotions
I am not made of steel
even if I was
steel also does melt

If we are in love
at all times we should remember
in bliss and in pain
our wish to be together
but when we forget
we are no longer in love
our I love you is hollow

I don't want to hurt
no. not anymore

let me be
and have your fun
free me to wander about
in search of my-self
in pursuit of the happiness
I once had

this pain is sucking
the last ounce of blood
from me
I don't want to die

free me
from your sweet sounding words
emancipate me
from your lascivious scent
and tantalising flesh
release me
from the shackles of your delights
I don't want to hurt

we must go our separate ways
yours a love lost
never to be recovered
mine a pain newly found
never to be forgotten
it is better this way
your life shall be happier
I hope our paths never cross

Part II

I did love you
you did not see
I love you now
you remain blind

in my secret thoughts
I embraced you
wished you well
even when I wandered astray
you were still there
so I came back
now I am here
but you are gone

in my hardships
you remained my pillar of strength
when I was lost
in you I was found
but now that I am found
it is you I lose

if only you could stay with me
a little longer
with me
decipher a new beginning
if only we can put aside
our selfish wants
and enjoy our togetherness
if only we could love again
in each other lose ourselves
with our arms embrace
feel the heat of our bodies together
and like young lovers
watching the beauty of the valleys
beneath the open skies
see the beauty in our eyes
and capture the love
in our hearts

Part III

maybe
maybe it is too late
and too much to ask
but how I wish you to come back
to be with me
and me with you.

if only you could say yes
if only it brings you back
if only it makes you happy
if only it shows you how much
you mean to me
how much I love you
I too will say
I want to go out with you

I wish this to be true
you with me
and me with you
if this dream could come true
I will not go astray
I will not lose you
I don't want to hurt
think of me as foolish
but I miss you

The Lord gave ...

it was only yesterday
when I met him
down in the shacks
of the East Bank
he was just a kid
today he is dead
I asked why
they said:
the Lord gave
and has taken away

I remember her
as the childless old woman
everyone called
the wicked old witch
yet no one knew her
not that we cared
now it is too late
for the Lord gave
and has taken away

just a snotty
glue-sucking filthy youth
rummaging through the city's dirt bins
she froze to death
sleeping in the same city streets
they still tell me
the Lord gave
and has taken away

they were ordinary and simple people
their guilt
to disagree with the system
the military junta hanged them
and everybody continues to say
the good Lord gave
and has taken away

along came the minister
wailing and weeping
his child committed suicide
and I said
the Lord gave
the Lord has taken away

Images of the dead[9]

a simple man of no particular origin
his a litany of ordinary pleasantries
pointing out parking to motorists
on that fateful Friday morning
composed and serene in his final moments
he lay wounded on the pavement
of the street he daily travailed
respectfully and shocked
Braamfontein crowds filed alongside
resembling a guard of honour
to a fallen hero
murmuring as if singing a national anthem
horns and screeching sounds of cars
imitating a twenty-one-gun salute
to a leader of impeccable pedigree

black-hair, khaki-clad
chubby looking young woman
flowers in her hand
sits under a lamp post
in a contemplative mood
seemingly lost in thought
she does not know
it is her last Friday in this complex
unaware it is her final departure
from the land of radio programmes
and friends
comrades in arms

we sit here
our heads bow in sorrowful memory
to bid farewell to one of our own
this time with greater certainty
of peace in her life
the peace and harmony she never had
the tranquillity she seemingly anticipated

9   *in memory of Deon (never got his surname) and Sue Hamilton.
    Deon, from Cape Town, worked the parking lots of
    Braamfontein – Johannesburg. He was stabbed to death by
    another parking attendant. Susan 'Sue' Hamilton, from New
    Zealand, was a radio producer for Ulwazi Educational Radio
    Project in Braamfontein. She was stabbed to death by her lover*

What if

what if the world you create
never was, is not
what if the world you destroy now
is the world which is
and what if you woke up one morning
found your present creation gone
and all that existed
was your destroyed past
but
what if the destroyed past
was your dreams
your hopes
your purpose in living

what if you thought you felt love
you knew it, had it
and what if that love is
what you never had
never shared

what if you had sex with someone
but what you did was make love to another
could it be, therefore,
that you had sex
yet, never made love
but what if it was love making
and not sex
honestly now
what if both sex, making love
and love, never existed, does not exist

Clouds of death

overpowering dark clouds of death
hover above the horizon
bidding the tormented soul to come
offering the tortured body rest
promising eternal comfort
an end to misery and suffering.
but, hesitantly,
everlasting bliss is postponed
another plunge into the tumultuous
depths of life taken
if not for the diver's sake
for the children, and
if not for them, for life's sake.
consistent and unwavering, however,
are the clouds of death
and like daggers they
stand ready to snap.
maybe the death clouds
aren't on the horizons
but at the doorstep
knocking and knocking on the heart

Mortality

oh! mother earth explain to us
these intricacies of life
the inexplicable events of our existence
yet inescapable realities of our being
at one minute a child is alive
in a split second the child is dead

mortality is a complex condition
when I ask why life ends
the answer is elusive
so I search for clarity in cyberspace
and seek comfort in religious words
and mythologies
to extend living

in the meaningful-meaninglessness
of the end of life
we grapple with its purpose
when young lives commit suicide
we beg for higher knowledge
but we find no answer
then we are thrown into utter despair
because we wish they spoke
we wish they confided in us

Such is life

when will you grasp
the teachings of nature
from the seasons
when will you learn
that it is only
when you feel the bitter cold of winter
that you wish for summer
or when you feel the scorching sun
in the wild wastelands of drought
that you long for spring rains
and to rest under the shade

only when something is gone
do we wish to find it
while it is with us
we take it for granted
at times we loath it
when it is out of sight
its spectacle shines
draws the eye of the admirer
only then is it appreciated
for only then is it known
for what it is
to itself and to others
if we are fortunate
as with the seasons
it will be for a short while
but maybe forever
like in death

Reflections of one who lost

Part 1: about the self

he lost all in this battle
for it was one in which
he gave of himself fully
his heart is left there
on the battlefield
riddled and ravaged
he knows what he lost
his faith, his friend, himself,
the past, the present and the future.

Part 2: about the other

the victorious knows not
he inherits a greater loss
he is ignorant of the past
in his glory of the present
he lives the illusionary future
unaware of the current
titanic wave just unleashed
forgetful that *the foot has no nose*[10]

the conquered who betrayed in battle
instead of solidarity you chose defection
troubled days await ahead
for the ancients say,
one must not shit in the well[11]

Part 3: the healing

the defeated fighter sits
watches. waits.
for now he will erase memories
of the war
from his heart and his mind
he will forget the friend
and the heart he lost
the blood on his body
he will wash
the scars and wounds
carefully nurse.

Part 4: moving on

a good battle it was
he exclaims
I gave my all
and my all I lost
no more these types of wars
I have no friend
I have no heart
I have bitter memories

in the midst of it all
he tries to share a smile
but his tears betray him
so he sighs
struck by the pain in his heart
then he mumbles
as if speaking to himself
only those who lose know loss

10 *a Sesotho idiom, leoto ha le na nko, meaning you never know what will happen to you or where you might end up*

11 *another Sesotho idiom, o se ke oa nyela seliba, meaning one must not mess a good thing they have. Similar to if one lives in a glass house one shouldn't throw stones*

Letter to a friend

I cry Mzala[12]
but you cannot see
because the wailing is inside
do not be fooled
by the twinkle in my eye
night after night
I drench my pillows with sobbing
at day-break
my weeping is in the heart
an internal hiss
so I wear a smile Mzala
however I cry

I hurt mzi, I hurt
the pain within is debilitating
it has a gradual movement
an accuracy that pricks the heart
like the tip of a sharp pin
touching the skin
this agony induces paralyses
my knees are lame
my body feels borrowed
I am a young man
in an old man's body
I am burdened
burdened Mzala; I am burdened.
at times death is enticing
suicide a seemingly immediate medicine
but I am down
not out

to lose your love is not fun
to be robbed of a companion
is no game Mzala
when you love fully
lose completely
disorientation creeps in
and a void develops
you ask questions
no answers come forth

*12 a Nguni word meaning cousin. It is also an affectionate way to
call a close friend*

To Lolo, from Lolo

now she has not time
when love was strong
she would come
amidst tight schedules
and family commitments

I used to anticipate her coming
my heart beating hard and fast
like conga drums summoning
royalty
I would bury my head
in her voluptuous bosom
like a tourist overwhelmed
by the pyramids of the pharaohs
in her embrace I felt surrounded
as if by the gigantic monuments
of Monomotapa[13]
when my lips would touch hers
soft as dew
my tongue criss-crossing
like the movements of a snake
my want would reach
incongruous heights
my hardness inside her
would melt like gold in fire
as she eclipsed me with her
thighs
while making silent noises
throughout her up-and-down
sideways movements

like the *stimela*[14] bound for Soweto
then our heat would fill the room
like the sun rays on a winter day
and our scent would be like
a fragrance
side by side we would sleep
then
tickle, joke, laugh, talk,
kiss and caress
then I would look into her sleepy eyes,
to meet the morning light

but now she is gone
in her departure she stole my heart
she took my joy away
but why Lolo
where are you now
how deaf can you be
how blind

13 *an ancient African republic whose ruins border Limpopo, South*
  Africa, and Zimbabwe
14 *isiZulu word for train*

When night comes

moody moods
blues take my life away
when night comes
darkness descends
upon my heart
and my wail shoots up
from my gut

when the sun goes down
it goes down with me
taking me deep into
annals of the grave
sinking and sinking
way beyond resilience
and courage

when the night descends
upon the earth
it covers my life
with thunderous clouds
of darkness and sorrow
then I wonder whose child
I will be
as it walks me through
the valley of death
and parades me among the dead

when the night descends
I wonder if tomorrow will come

If my eyes
will see the morning light
when the night comes
I despair

In the silence of their hearts

if I could write better
I would express
the beauty and pain
of their life

if oratory was my gift
I would tell their stories
from generation to generation

if I could sing
my lyrics and melody
would enchant the listener

it is to them
in the silence of their hearts
I send this message

in their hearts
they search
in their innermost beings
they wonder
longing to find love
they never fail to love
for they love life
more than self
with their being
in harmony with humanity
their spirits
one with nature

Imaginations

imagine we are
in a different world
it belongs to us
in its plains
I am yours
and you are my breath
like children we play
grow up together
we become close
and come to know each other
what if your imagination is a dream
you wake up
to see the truth in your face
what if in the dream we clasp together
feel each other
and enjoy our company

then one night you went to bed
sunk into a deep sleep
went for a long walk
next to every step you take
a separate set of footprints shows
and an inner voice
told you they are mine
but you cannot see me

imagine in your sleep
you feel my presence
my arms around yours
our twig-like legs caressing

your shiny dark eyes
hovering on mine
our lips gently teasing
emotions of love espousing

then you rise from your sleep
your long walk comes to an end
you find I was always there

The movement (nostalgia)

we come from afar
our faces sun scorched
we have walked long distances
our bodies smell and drip with sweat
we trudged many roads
our feet are frozen from frost
treacherous alleys and valleys
we traversed
springs, streams and rivers
we crossed
on bended knee
mountain, hill, plain
were conquered
with our tormented
yet determined spirits
we stormed ahead
at times
the journey got long and bitter
sometimes
short and joyous
then our crushed bones
would be revive
our resilience unparalleled
our voices would reach
a crescendo
through melodies
of tragic-melancholic-joyful song
accompanied by the razzle-dazzle
rhythmic thumping of the feet
as it meets the solid
silent rock of earth
suddenly brought to life

in the fiery greyish-brown
approval ascent
of the ground

suddenly
tear, mucus, smiles
mix
as memory of our past
present and future
conjure vivid atrocious realities
we trudge on
in this long journey
bound with the spirit of the dead
courageously nurturing
and pressing us ahead
the fearless hope of the living
dares us ever
amidst terror, trauma and pain,
in the heart of isolation and separation
our human goal gained us friends
far from our point of origin
far from our mothers' wombs

we come from afar
to reach this point
our movement never failed us
even when times were lean and mean

at times
the movement was like
torrential rains
accompanied by thunder and lightning
ravaging through the land
sometimes

like an overflowing river
it would amass itself
even with unnecessary load
only to rid itself of it
at an opportune time
expansive like the ocean
letting in all the streams
our journey would be ordinary
but human
yet our goal noble

a nomadic people
purposeful in our journey
simple in our presentation
humble in our request
uncompromising in our quest
that is who we are
a people born of hardship
tried and tested by a long
sojourn in far distant isles
brought to rest by an unwavering
determination for common good

the journey has not ended
the movement continues
only a temporary rest is permitted

ja, mense
ons is van ver af[15]
we still have to move on
because miracles of today
surpass failed dreams of yesterday

15 *Afrikaans for; indeed, people, we come from far*

Lonesome nights

another sleepless night
another endless night
whose end is abrupt
except for the tension that torments
the lonesomeness
that keeps me awake
generating the warmth
that longs for affection
in this desolation
someone's presence is felt
right here
by my side
a strange but teasing
tranquillity befalls
and gladness fills
my soul
because
even on this lonely vigil
I feel your presence
right here
by my side

Things you do

initially I cried
believing
in your humanity
like a newly born baby
I wept
hoping to be spared your misery
instead you grinned at me
like an old corpse
while you spread me
as if I were a rugged carpet
and you found immense pleasure
in my desperation

initially I felt pain
as you carelessly
strutted about watching me die

even then
you still said
I relish the moment

what was once my heart
is numb

my head is covered in shame
I hide my face
lest people read from its deep lines
I bury my sorrow in silence
to avoid being called derogatory names
still you sink
into the gutter
of your haughty parade

Inhumanity

from place to place
shifting and moving ceaselessly
neither a hello nor a goodbye
lepers in their places of birth
they turned out to be
old neighbourhoods
become death camps..
that's when humanity
became inhuman

from old to young
a people made into a human experiment
supposed showers
turned human gas killers
dumping sites becoming open graves
to bodies of men, women and children
no names
neither dignity nor a deserved final respect
just a countless human carcass
victims of open death policies
and genocides..
humanity became inhuman

mortal remains everywhere
 paid respect to by vultures
without rest
their spirits
mindlessly roam about
interfering with the living
our hands bloodstained with
indifference to their plight

their names remain written
in stone
as a memory..

they were once
Germans not Jews
Africans not *kaffirs*[16]
Rwandese not Tutsis or Hutus
they were humans
living in one global village
but then
humanity turned inhuman

*16 a derogatory term used by white South Africans against the
Black, particularly African, population. Similar to whites in the
USA calling African-Americans nigger*

The dry season of life

an unfortunate time
a generation of non-visionaries
without courage
to confront their present
strung to failed attempts
of arresting the future
through temporary drunken states
of bliss
neither here nor there
except for a handful of dollars
exchanging with the finger-licking
snow-white powder sniffing
that turns images into existential truths
a vicious cycle
of no entry points and no exit
truly
things are not the way
they used to be
and this
I'm afraid
is the dry season of life

Immigration

throngs hurriedly
held in a perilous
single minded exodus
from their place of birth
 hopes and dreams
for a better world
suspended in cash
en route to prison or death

southward bound hordes
illegally cross
Beit Bridge[17] on foot
taming the Musina[18] crocs
in quiet haste for Jozi via Polokwane[19]

northward bound
they row raging waves
for the European shores
sometimes they make
a daring dart
across the blistering sand
for the Arabian oil rigs
some burrow underground tunnels
in flight from the Mexican tortilla
to the American dream
guarded by the Texas ranger

this is a human trail of starvation
escaping perdition
with its nightmare of hunger

held in bondage
between making for the border post
and dying in destitution
while politicians elucidate
endless plans
about millennium goals
they are yet to score
for human solidarity

a human convoy
in commune with famine
afraid of death
hurriedly runs away
in the hope that another war
never comes
praying that another despot
is not born

17 *official border crossing between South and Zimbabwe*
18 *South African town in the north, near the Zimbabwe border*
19 *the capital city of the Limpopo province in the North of South*
   Africa. Formerly known as Pietersburg. Jozi is a popular slang
   name for the famous, populous city of Johannesburg – or
   Joburg, in South Africa

Trains with my dreams

bits of my dream leave the station
with each train that rides past
I sit alone on this empty bench
my hopes rise
with another screeching
that arrives on the platform
thinking you will be
among the passengers
but my dream fades
when the whistle blows

The mourners

like a theatrical act
when the curtain rolls
and performers
conclude their final scene
dust flies off the spades
into to the open earth
where his silent body
lies inside the wooden chamber
we stand huddled together
in collective sorrow
our eyes holding back tears
as we watch light fade
with the departure
of one of our own
then in a solemn march
we return home
to wash our hands
and cleanse the spades
knowing we will not
see him again

African woman

celebrate her
from birth to death
she is there without fail
nurturing and cuddling
unselfishly
bearing the pain
and carrying the burden
celebrate the African woman

celebrate her child
celebrate her
in times of war
she hides your face from the foe
in bitter days
she confronts Goliath
celebrate the African woman

celebrate her child
celebrate her
in the bush where she fell
and in the streets
where she was mowed down
pay your respects
at the foot of the Union Buildings[20]
build a monument in her memory
celebrate the African woman

celebrate her child
celebrate her
from Moutse to Qumbu
Kuruman to Weenen[21]

across the entire landscape
sing the song of praise
to this porter who shapes us
the sister, lover and daughter
above all mother – at times father
who bore and bears humiliation
celebrate the African woman

20 *the government buildings in Tshwane (Pretoria), in South Africa,*
   where the Executive resides and works. This is where the famous
   women's march against the pass laws was in 1956. They
   delivered a memorandum to the then apartheid President
21 *names of towns in the provinces of Limpopo/Mpumalanga,*
   Eastern Cape, Northern Cape and KwaZulu-Natal, in South
   Africa

Untitled

One

imagine fireflies flying
their torch lighting
the open skies
such is your smile.
imagine their bright
shimmering flame
brightening the vastness
of the night,
such is your soul

Two

for some life is treachery
a continued denial of happiness
a permanent existence
of failed dreams
and daily encounter with loss
whatever love they find
whatever beauty they meet
never last

Three

see the sun
coming to a close
and all that remains
is your hand in mine
picture the world
coming to an end
and all I see is your face
imagine all dreams
shattered
and one that stands
is ours

Four

in my mind I still see you
and hold your face
in my illusory walk
your hand
steadily holds my stagger
in my imagined
and real space
your smile warms my heart

Five

think of me kindly
as I do of you
so that as I walk
among the crowds
my mind entangled with thoughts
of leaving you behind
my will to return
would express my love
for life

Six

fear enslaves
until it chokes life
from within the living
the shiver of colds
freezes the summer
in our hearts
and the fearful fall
at the feet
of the altar of love

Seven

how many times
should we fall in love
to know we love
to know we are loved
what can we tell of love
that love hasn't done
or revealed about us
is it our hope to live long
so we can see
the face of love
how do we know
that we will recognise it then

Eight

please don't explain
it is best left like this
do not call me
at least for a while
you can post a letter
so by the time it reaches me
my heart would have mended
but then
what is my address

Nine

how should we define cruelty
what of hurt
is it in the amount of time
one endures suffering
or is it in the inflicting of pain
maybe pain is desire
or longing

Ten

English skies weep with me
their salty downpour
taste the jealous rage
that muted you and
in turn
sliced my tongue

Eleven

in your radiant eyes
I seek your depths
eagerly I plough
through your hidden maze
only to be dazed
by your inviting allure

Twelve

I smile
to ease the sorrow
inside me
I stroll in the drizzle
to free the tears in my eyes
my yell is louder
it comes from the deep hollow
in me
I use slippery words
to hide the yearning in my heart

Thirteen

complications of time and space
like ocean waves
come crushing
onto my fragile emotions
I wish I could hold the clock
I wish I could narrow the distance

Fourteen

in darkness I shall vanish
in blackness my veins shall rise
in this profane insanity
fame and fortune reside to fade

Fifteen

touch and feel the anger
wrapped in this solidity
seeking to free itself
from the ardour
of raviollied walls
which widen
only to fold
in an exclaimed gift
without words

Sixteen
my jailor is imprisoned
by his bitterness
watching me
stroll to my freedom
to evade the passage of history
he is locked
in the memory of the power
he once had
in his fear
he breeds hate
to scorn the smile
in my open arms

Seventeen
kiss me before I die
so that my lips can taste
of the sweetness of life before death
embrace me before I am deceased
so that my body can abound
in fresh fragrances
as I take counsel with decay

Eighteen
you did not say
you were leaving
your eyes never told
of your impending departure
except to ensnare me
in love's gaze
so secret was your move
that your kiss
concealed the separation

Nineteen

the gods were generous with beauty
when they made you
the graciousness of how
they moulded you
appears in your sleep
when I tiptoe to you lay
by your side
my step falters
and I fall
only to be greeted by your smile
that welcomes me with a kiss
my arm draws
the contours
of your well shaped body
my lips gently caress your flesh
my mouth fills with your salty fluids
then I feel your feet
clutch on my bare back
drawing me in deeper
and deeper
into you
my mind is hazy
as I swallow you whole
your soft murmur
is like a prayer that crescendos
until we both rise
and collapse into each other's
embrace
I remain inside you
feeling the playful twitches
your body makes
finally my want totally

dissipates
the room fills with
fragrances of your aroma
and the beautiful shine
on the face
that welcomes me with a kiss

Twenty
winter clings on
in the crisp of spring
festivities summon the blossom
soon the sky will play the fire dance
behind the rumble
so the children could bathe
in the open
before the sun bakes
their bodies again
then I hear giggling voices
of children
I know I am home
I am safe

Twenty-one
each time I see you
I thirst for you
I am ceased by a fiery desire
that yearns to burn
inside the secrets beneath
your robes
I want to know you
search your heart
to reveal the person
you hide from me
to lay bare your soul
so once again
you learn to love
as I love you
so the loneliness we feel
could fade
and the walls that surround us
crumble

Twenty-two
loneliness is anguish
in this moment
of bliss
when life feels sweet
it is death
I find enticing

Twenty-three

stay with me a little while
so your voice could lighten
the heaviness of my heart
hold me a little more
so the moonlight
could brighten my soul
pray with me a while longer
so in my solitude
the gods can hear my prayer

Twenty-four

sometimes life seems
to pass me by
with a thump
then I wrestle with the dark
that inhabit me
imploring the devil
to seek me out for a duel
as I sink in this deep dying hole
my mind constantly shifts
to each traumatic memory
I wish to forget forever

Twenty-five

the day is long
the gods
will not leave me
they won't take me either
my heart is disturbed
time holds it to ransom
where the old clock stands still

Twenty-six

aspire to love
at all times
I am prepared to love
ask why
I don't know
except for this
it is in loving that we are
it is in being that we love

take heed and notice
love will break you down
yet it will build you up
love will shred you into pieces
yet it will mend your heart

in love
you are like a child
you act and speak
like a child
and it is there where you mature
foolish you may be
this is how you gain wisdom
only the wise know love
how to be broken down
and built up
to be scattered
and gathered together again
how to be lost
and found

Twenty-seven
homeless
jobless
penniless

I could use a drink
maybe a puff
to send clouds of smoke
or drive some dizzy spell
into my nerve
just to escape reality
only for a while

rummaging through newspapers
classified pages
job adverts
interviews

like the homeless
lining up soup kitchens
waiting
learning to wait
waiting for tomorrow
I wait

Twenty-eight
my drum beats to the pulse
of your heart
with your every move
my yearning bursts in gushes
of impassioned desire
so I rise
in a feeble attempt to catch
my escaping breath

Twenty-nine
between your eyes and mine
a torrent
that blesses the bliss
in our hearts

between your lips and mine
sheaths and sheaths
of joyful showers
awash with honey juices
from your flesh

inside your body and mine
playful embraces
turn into love's eternal baths

in your veins and mine
streams
become life's bearer of love

on your lips and mine
a raindrop
of plentiful kisses

Thirty
my tired eyes awake
with your birth
the tiny bundle you are
speaks of the freshness of life
which revives
my numb mind
and tingles my lame body
the birth of new life
breathes life once more

Thirty-one

my silent thoughts torture me
when images of your silent smile
flicker past my mind
the quietness of my soul
brings me no joy
when I ponder what
became of us
and the things that
have brought us apart

I sit
in the secluded corner
of my inconsolable world
lonely and desolate
wishing you could hold me
touch me
so that I can again be admired
love again
and share this moment
with you

Thirty-two

your radiant eyes
draw me closer into you
in my eagerness to find you
I search through your maze
then devour each supple fruit
that grows in your
secret garden

Thirty-three
I smile to placate
the sorrow I feel inside
I walk in the drizzle
to free the tears
which cover my face
I yell loud
hoping I could drown the sadness
I speak in a silvery tongue
to conceal the longing
in my heart

Thirty-four
silently and with ease
she moved into my life
a beacon of hope
when I despair
in my dreary world
she is the expression of beauty
yet she cannot see
my good intentions for her
her fear to open up
means she won't know
that I care
that I love her

Soul mate

Babo

please not that song
because
memories of her waning smile
and her fading face
under the stylish hat
that hides the lifeless eyes
visibly flood my mind

please not that song
it reminds me
of when she left
by then
she had abandoned
the will to live
little did I know
that when I came
to say goodbye
she had foretold her funeral
before my arrival

please do not play that song
it recalls emotions
when her eyes welled with tears
'don't touch', she said
lest your embrace
evoke the pain in my aching flesh
at least what remains of it

here at this very spot
her body had

twisted and turned
contorted
under the gaze of the street lamp
in spell-bound exultation
to make an unmentionable offering

so please
not that song

I remember the children
the children
in their perfected ritual glance
yes the children...
what to tell them now

I ask you
don't play that song please
not that song

it makes me recall
it makes me see
when the soul
is dislodged from the body
on this ground
where once
a gun was raised to my head
and we were made to lie face down
on the frosty earth
as the hijacker made for our car
that day she lived
she had soul
she wanted to live
and today ... eish!

just don't play that song
please ...

images of a once vibrant life
tumbling into extinction play out
a champion for life
now cursed by death's fatal touch
whittling away in fear
covered up in shame
in the hollow shell of her body
her breath trapped
making slow passages
in the lonely wait for death
friends not wanted

in the quiet
of my suffering heart
I wish she knows
I love her
for even now
long after her hour
I make a fruitless attempt
to will her on
as I see glistening fountains
on her brown face
then in solemnity
my heart hums
that dreaded chant
so please don't play that song

My song

you are the song I sing
when I am alone
I sing of my longing for you
and of my wish to be in your arms
each time we are apart
I doubt if we will
ever be together
then I sing your name
in a song of love

What will you do?

what will you do
when the light fades
from your eyes
and darkness befalls
your world
what will you do
when your heart
no longer holds
and all that remains
is the past what you once were
what will you do
when the joy you thought you had
is a mere wish list
that burdens your heart
what will you do
when love is not palpable
in your night companion
who once sent nightmares away
what will you do
when the heat waves of the heart
make way
for the cold winters of the soul
what will you do
when your hopes and dreams
crumble
on the love
you thought you found

Life fades

grains of sand slip through fingers
such is this life
a collection of a material world
disappearing
like the once dense clouds of fog
in the clearing tumultuous seas
holding the secret troubles
of tormented hearts
whose footprints are washed
along the sandy beach
by waves
and gushing winds
and like the seagull
whose flight
sometimes comes crushing
against the rocks
only to float like a radar-less sailor
upon the roaring waters
the soul yearns to soar
before life ends
like granules of sand
life slips through
and like clouds of fog
it all dissipates

Sacred ritual

outstretched arms
held in lofty heights
making a personal sacrifice
the wet tongue
teasingly quells the burning
in the fiery canal
while tuned in
to a joyfully hummed chant
clasped together in union
an offer of self
is made through graceful motion

Oom Bey[22]

on a cold day of my spring
another mighty oak
is struck to the ground
and like the giants that preceded it
it quietly slips out
of this life
yet the earth feels
the thunder of its landing

22 *the affectionate way Reverend Dr Beyers Naude, the Dutch
Reformed Church's minister and fierce anti-apartheid Afrikaner
activist, was called among comrades. Oom means uncle. Oom
Bey, like Bram Fischer, endured a great deal of suffering and
marginalisation from the Afrikaner community and the
apartheid regime because of their support for the liberation
struggle*

Desolation

my dreams
have forgotten me
I am resigned to the company
of my unforgiving soul
night and day
I walk aimless
as time goes by

Farewell to Shenge[23]

so I lay myself down
with a heavy heart
reports of his violent death
in contrast with his gentle demeanour
he moves on
to the other life with ease
his cat-like footsteps
like snapshots
on the shiny wooden tiles
his spirit lingers on
in his careful knock
on my third-floor
office door

23 *Shenge is the clan name of the Buthelezi. Wilkies Buthelezi was
an organiser and coordinator of the energy sector in the
National Union of Mineworkers (NUM). He was found brutally
murdered by the roadside. He was on his way to Johannesburg,
from Mpumalanga*

Dreadlocked dance

in the dark
bohemian bedroom
her dreads dance
her skin glows
with aromatic oils
feeling the palpable airwaves
of her endowments
I swing on her dreadlocks
in concert
to her harmony

Just a good night wish

for once a star shines bright
through the dark veld of life
as the path rises before you
carrying you into the homely fires
where love awaits you
now I sleep in peace
knowing
that I sleep in your heart

All smiles

I'm still smiling
because the wonder
of your being
envelopes my life
I'm still smiling
because the dance
in your walk
intoxicates my gaze
I'm still smiling
because the splendour
of your love
finds faith in me

I remember

You said
"I want you not to forget"
so I remember
but memories only serve
to engender lonesomeness
still I don't forget
though the reason for remembrance
is so distant

Paranoid

we live in a strange world
all around me
the powerful
are gripped by a siege mentality
free speech is at a premium
and so it is that
in these streets
shades of dim and light
shelter the shady
and grey is
the only clarity

Soulful conversions

the high priestess
who conquers hearts
makes me a sip
from her holy chalice
she washes me in her
steamy basins
and spreads my flesh
with scented ointments
a whispering hushed prayers
in my ear
she moves with patient and
abruptly spirited swings
that intoxicate me
delirious I thrust into her sanctuary
and explode in its secret chamber
then she lays her palm
on my perspiring head
with a smile
extracting the last vestiges
of my vanquished soul

Rejection

now that we are found
you wish to leave
as I seek to discover you
you evade my touch

The call to love

once more
for the love of love
we plough
these paths
of human existence
and intimate relations
so that
to the call to love
we can reply with our life

Ruined hopes

streets that
were once my pride
stand paved
with skeletons
of the witless faithful
who sing praises
to chariots of the mighty
wheeling past
towards palaces of power
while truth and justice
attempt to stand guard
on pavements
of a shackled freedom
as signposts of love
are overturned

Woman rise!

rise up boisterous woman
the sun shines
on your slumber-ridden eyes

rise up courageous woman
your body
signifies a resilient composite
that's your soul

rise up woman of weary heart
so you may live
to love once more

Maybe

you should have waited
for summer
because sunshine has means
of penetrating dark clouds
maybe then
your mood would have lifted
from the gloom

Lover's lies

they stand together
pretending to be one
clasped in each other's arms
living a dream
that never was

Eclipsed

abandoned by the light god
my life momentarily wanders
through the passage of darkness
exposing me to the sorcery
of bloodthirsty vampires
I wish not to fall prey
of their snares
and in this moment
of my vulnerability
give sway to the ever-present
temptation to terminate
my life

Namaste

so that sounds of sirens
do not drown
the voices of Seth, Mayakovsky
and Mother Teresa
... *namaste!*

so that records of injustice
do not replace
the novels of love, laughter and dance
... *namaste!*

so that the violence of the street
doesn't wash away
the enchanting colour of life
... *namaste!*

that the deity
I salute in you
brings rhythm
to the discord of daily living
... *namaste!*

England

this land is so cold
smiles freeze on our faces
our usually warm exchanges
become icy
customary courtesies
the coldness of snow
makes our step heavy
this land is so cold
the sun hides
behind the clouds
a darkness and gloom abounds
then my heart dreams
of the stars
in the open skies
of my home

Ghetto-ised!!

it hurts
hunger pangs growl
inside our hollow bellies
it hurts

naked babies
wondering around
parent-less
flies swooping in
on their mucus laden noses
while they scream like
sirens during the beer raid
it hurts

collapsing shelters
in urine-river pathways
it hurts...

every birth a death
every death a birth
a vice versa
vicious cycle of life
it hurts...

Lonely hearts

they continue to dance
pretending they do not hear
their music fell silent
and their rhythm is lost
they continue to dance
as if they do not know
their harmony is no more
that their concert is ended

The dreamer

wanderer of lost worlds
tread where you shall meet
new people
so by day
you may learn
in the words of strangers
and by nightfall
be wise
from the dreams you weave

seeker of new paths
walk no further
without guide in your soul
so if you go astray
you may finally find
the road that leads
to your next home

explorer of treasures
look not far
 away from your heart
where you shall find
the road that leads
to new discoveries

oh! seeker of truth
search no further
than your heart

foolish one
dream new dreams
lest your mind goes stale
your body goes frail
and your soul dies

Tomorrow

the heart sprints
into tomorrow
the feet fly
so the hopeful mind
can touch the horizon
the spirit soars
like an eagle
to see beyond
the horizons

Leru le letso[24]

ghastly winds rage
firepower lightning
adorns the heavens
stormy clouds are held
in a grumbling convocation
the sea of blackness
marches in sounds of fury

24 *dark clouds, the storm*

Enchanted!

my heart leaps
like a throng
of ululating women
welcoming the bride

Love potion

the bug bit no further
than the heart
sultry lips put a spell on me
a sip from the potion
left me inebriated

The mating game

steam rises
between elevated human pillars
of intensely pounding exchanges
silky-milky waterfalls
make their way
through the narrow stream
into the open-mouthed
welcoming sea
dewy lips pat hardened nipples
as foggy eyes
of a palm
touch the brow in tender
selfless offering

Questions of love

why is love
perhaps loving
so confusing
could it be
I mean
just maybe
that love
is confused

What if?

as I said then
what if
summer never came
will you go room to room
in search of warmth
then you find bliss
but no soul
and no passion
then you remember
when I said
what if
your summer never came

Asparagus risotto

your delectable dish
I have tasted
its aroma
pulled me off the sidewalk

an array of seasoning
concealed the potion
poisoning my palate
hmmm
my mouth is watering
my whet appetite
cannot restrain the compulsion
as I devour of your delights
and sample more
from your warm delicious gifts

Good night

as the final flicker is swallowed
by the belly of darkness
I blow a good night kiss
your way
to ease the groans of longing
my imagined touch
which is a yearning today
rushes the birth of tomorrow
so I can be next to you

Ten days – one side

day in and day out
I wait with anticipation
mindless with want
holding on to my memories
with each hour that passes
these moments of separation
feel eternal

Ten days – other side

my eyes feel
heavy with sleep
my arm is lame from scribbling
the print on the letters
is becoming faint
along with the fading ink
yet my hand is consumed
by an urge
to pen these words
I write until dawn
until the last word
on the final page

Silly

in my morning daze
your serene countenance
flew in with the bird choir
that interrupted the tranquility
of my last dream
as the rays freed
the leaf from the dew

On Jules' Street

that night
our souls kissed
under the neon lights
a joyful wave
seized your mourning
causing our bodies
to move in concert
to the Afro-beat
luring us
to each other
in an act of rebirth
blending the distant suns
of 'Maletsoai-Jozi[25]
with the rain clouds
of Scarborough-York
in an unforgettable bond
of friendship

25 *Maletsoai is a small town in the North-East of the Eastern Cape province - it is formally known as Aliwal-North. Jozi is slang (called tsotsi-taal in South Africa) for Johannesburg*

Golden dreams

at peace my child at peace
the demons are silenced
sleep well now baby sleep well
the full moon
in her magical gentleness
and silver glow
brightens your dream world
sleep now child sleep
the spirits wait to caress you
sleep well now my baby sleep well

End of beginnings

you do not call me anymore
so too my urge to ring you
wanes
even when we are together
our playful games
and verbal exchanges
under the covers
cease

Forbidden fruit

I do not wish to stop
playing with your head-long silk
and brush your neck
when our faces meet
in the smiley planes
adjoining our ears
I do not want to stop
wrapping myself around you
pretending to be a violinist
on your outstretched arm
I do not dream to stop
being bumped by your teasing hip
on High Street
and giggle
as I dance
from your fingers

Coconut delights

my untold desire
to hurl this tormented shell
at your embrace
to take a plunge
in your tantalising delights
my tongue dribbles with their sap
with each searching dive
into your layers
with every dip
I probe your hidden sanctuary
conquering
and calming
its temperamental
convulsive contractions
as I go under
and come up
I feel born again
then for a moment
I die a blissful death
in my delightful deliriousness
I bid your open arms to arrest me
and appeal to your hugging legs
to free me
while I genuflect adoringly
my eyes in awe of the bounty
decked before me
taste me
penitent and intercessor
 whispering in harmony
taste me

the tempo of the chant rises
urging the fire in us
until it reaches a crescendo
that unleashes hot streams
then we succumb into
each other's embrace
drops running down our bodies
as the soft spring rains
I do not know what world this is
I do not know if this moment is now
or it never existed
until the light comes through
the window pane
and meets your smile

Palestine skies

Fire flies
explode above the heads
of children
dark nights
with fearful babies
in desperate arms
wailing mothers
huddle in the corner
of a dying wall

Anticipation

knowing that I will see you
surpasses the sadness
I feel when I miss you
I overcome the loneliness
at this moment
knowing that I love you
now and always
bears today's dream
of tomorrow

Black smile

clapping thunder of blackness
ascends from the smoke
in smiles that cry freedom
through red tongues
soaring golden skies
glistening streams
from the eyes
that spring pools
to bathe the black
and brown children
it blends with a mamba's strike
that breeds terror in the hood
it is the face
that bears the brunt of pain
but beams a smile
that captivates

Msawawa,²⁶ my love

between us there's only a chasm
because of dreams
I weave for you

a lonely heart
with tears of contrition bathes
to atone this moment of separation
it is for love of you
I brave these planes
of skies that soak my skin
and swallow the sun
how I long for the caress
from your golden glow
that blinds me in ecstasy
as the rays penetrate
this blackness at dawn

Between us there's only a chasm
because of dreams
I weave for you

I pray the gods
to take my soul
to spare me this desolation
then I invoke the spirit
for courage
so that once more
I adorn you with jewels
upon your bosom
oh how I yearn

to touch your brown flesh
that gives birth to children
and buries them in their youth

between us there's only a chasm
because of dreams
I weave for you

eyes swell with wells
craving to hear your sounds
this countenance
clothed in smiles from the soul
where disarming grace
belies the bare brute of breeding
my desire to be seduced
by swaying hips of rainbow plumage
that sometimes blends
in the Madiba dance

between us there's only a chasm
because of dreams
I weave for you

my excitement sprints ahead
to be draped in white robes
of the Maloti
your delights are plentiful
my mouth salivates with appetisers
which abound at the foot
of your mountainous table
your passion is a rising heat wave
momentarily dowsed

just so you can teasingly intoxicate
with your earthen aroma

Between us there's only a chasm
because of dreams
I weave for you

26 *slang term for South Africa, sometimes used to mean Soweto -
the most famous South African black township. The term plays
on the notion of the 'south'*

She never came

revellers gather
their chatter of anticipation
ascends along the concert hall
in each smile my wait grows
while the ticket claws in my pocket
to the strings of the kora
that ushers the performers
on the stage
the audience's ululation
to the rapturous sound
of the trumpet
lifts my fading hope in defence
against the vacant spot
in my company
on the last note
my fingers clasp the ticket
in a final bid to stall
the passage of time
from a dying dream
the music ends
the dancers go
except puddles
with after show hangers-on
then in the English drizzle
that bemoans
in a drowning heart
I take a solitary step
towards my slumber
With dreams burdened
by the ticket
inside my pocket

No goodbyes

only weep for me
when I'm dead
for then you know for certain
I won't come
except in dreams
preserved for the spirit world
wait for me
wait for me until I return
because our distance
is measured
with thoughtful memories
just as our time apart
hums to the clock
from a longing heart

Old hands

these old hands of mine
frail
mould faces of infants
these old hands
with a tremble
bathe bare bodies
these old hands
wrinkled
clasp in intercession
these old hands
elevate in hope
for the glimmer in your eyes
these old hands
that stroke and caress carefully
these old hands of mine
frail
yet create and recreate

Come and dance

I accept to dance with you
I feel we have danced before
but then the music was not flowing
for we were inspired
by different lyrics

today when we dance
I can hear the breathing
in your breasts
and touch the movement
in your veins
as your body joyfully moves
with mine

with every stroke of the instruments
my wish
is to stay glued to this floor
so we can dance
until the morning comes

Matla![27]

the golden glow
embraces the naked blackness
its glimmer in the blue skies
gives rise to hope
in the bare footed toddler
braved by the bullet
that grazed his face
to restore the smile
that screamed *Mayibuye!*[28]
with a clenched salute
black power

27 *power, strength. It is usually a call by the liberation movement,
in particular in the Congress Movement, to symbolise unity and
collective strength by raising the fist*
28 *come back; a call for the return of the land to the Africa people*

Hopeless-ness

my soul is troubled
I am weary of living
my heart looks for comfort
in forbidden passages
and alleyways
where flesh is sold
and its joy is stale
in my despair
I have given up
on wanting to live

A simple wish

just a simple wish
to hear your voice
so even though
physically apart
I can feel your presence
call me
so the miracle of telephony
can transport us
to each other's hold
transform these anxious moments
of loneliness
into real dreams
for our union

3700 kilometres

even this far
three thousand
seven hundred kilometres away
you touch me
at this very moment
hell cannot hold
the lunging flames
from my longing heart
three thousand
seven hundred kilometres away
I know I will see you soon

Let go

I left you
so I can find myself
and learn to love again
your lies broke my trust
your cheating robbed me
of my highly prized treasure
your flirting affair
stole my secret
intimate moments with you

you betray me
then you wish to see me
yet when you delighted
in the arms of your newfound lover
my affection was not good enough
for you

when we were together
I loved you
with all my heart
and I believe I have loved you
long enough
if I stay one minute longer
it will be spiteful
then I will resent you

it is time to let me go
now my songs are laments
which I play
in the company
of broken hearts
to console myself

Before the flight home

lie here with me
let me rest my head
in your bosom
so when the moment arrives
you can fly with me
inside your heart
do not leave me yet
soothe my breasts
with the ever gentle
circling movements
from your hand
give me that mouth to mouth aid
so I can share the air you inhale
stay clasped to me like this
so that I can feel
the bulge of that masculinity
as you perform each individual rite
to exorcise my epileptic fits
whose rage is tamed
in the thick warm stream
that flows through us now
do not let the big bird
fly with you
and take you away from me
this rite of passage
must not end
even when dawn
comes to take you away

Betrayal mzala

I wish to hate her
instead I love her
she has left me
with an emptiness inside me
it hurts so much
my skin is numb
I can no longer feel
the touch of the sun
my eyes do not wish
to see the beauty
of a woman's face
as her lover strokes her cheeks
my heart wants to forget
how it feels to be held
my tears have
dried up

What went wrong?

your bright star
is losing its shine
your once alluring lustre
chokes the freedom
you gave up so much for
the haughty parade
of might at the marketplace
that once stood as a rendezvous
for all
is disgraceful
now you burn down homes
of those who visit your land

Monument of life

it lives as a memory
in those who pass on
or maybe dare to live on
like a flickering flame
in the dead of night
it gives direction

Sketches of the south

Freedom

give us our freedom
because until then
we will flirt with death
where we are laid
myths will rise
and legend sprout

Young lives

my old sages
used to say
ukuzala ngukuzolula[29]
because their pride and future
lived in their young
today
men in fatigues
clutching automatic rifles
on armoured trucks
crush our seed
and bury it
before it grows

29 *an isiXhosa idiom meaning that raising children is a guarantor
for parents in their old age, they will be cared for*

Come walk with me

take my hand
and walk with me
together we can meet
tomorrow's challenge

today we must walk
hand in hand
yesterday
we chose separate paths
we sent the children to battle
yours to kill mine
after I raised them
mine to blow up yours
after crossing great rivers

to know you is my wish
that I may live with you
side by side
and together
a new neighbourhood build

treacherous seas
we have conquered
dangerous paths tread
now an unknown world
must be vanquished
and we together
must do it

the past our past
is gone

but not forgotten
bridges of friendship and trust
burnt and destroyed
but the ruins remain
yes we have seen
terrible things
but now
it is good tidings we want
if not for us
for our children

what do we have to lose
that is not lost already
the future is unknown
yet
it awaits us
come
take my hand
and walk with me

the present demands
that we be companions
that together
we should conquer our fears
without guilt
without shame

come
ready or not
we must walk
hand in hand

All in the name[30]

oh! what names these places have
what names
filled with echoes
of beauty and splendour
ever calling the stranger to see
but
how contradictory their events
how unpalatable
the experiences of their dwellers

Sweetwaters in the valley has turned sour
it is red with blood that flows in it
leaving no drop for cooking or drinking
even none for the young
to swim in its streams

Imbali is withering
from the stench of dead bodies
suffocating from the smell of human blood
ever choking from gun-smoke and
army tanks that pass by day

eMpumalanga the sun sets
its warmth covered with chill
in the human heart
its shining splendour and rays
clouded with
cries of children and mothers
and forlorn burning tyres
on the road

no sweet waters in the streams
no imbali to admire
and no sunrise in this valley

but I know
that one day
sweet waters will spring from the fountains
to wet the withering imbali
the romantic aroma of the rose will fill us
with its fragrance
and the daffodils
will twinkle in our eyes

that day
from empumalanga the sun will shine
majestic in splendour
its rays dispelling the dark clouds
hovering over us
its warmth chasing away
the cold chill in our hearts

30 Imbali, Sweetwaters and eMpumalanga (Hammersdale) are
   townships in Pietermaritzburg (eMgungundlovu) and around
   the KwaZulu-Natal midlands. Imbali means flower;
   Mpumalanga means where the sun rises

In memory of

when she died hanging washing
he returning from school
but never reached home
when they died in the train
to their workplace
when they were mowed down
queuing at the rank

in memory of
when he slipped to death
on a piece of soap
in the shower
when he hanged himself
in a prison cell
when he jumped
from the fourteenth floor
of a maximum security prison

in memory of
when they were hanged
in Central Prison[31]
stools loose
and eyes popped out
hacked maimed murdered
shot
while playing running singing
praying struggling sitting
in memory of their denied existence

in memory of
when they were raped

in the streets
the abused
and sexually molested child
struggling to grow
the woman bruised and broken
by the very one
who claimed to love her
the farmworker
who was whipped chained to a tree
their story unknown
they endure their pain in silence
in memory of their battered bodies
in memory of their shattered self-esteem.

in memory of
the glue-sucking youngster
living the illusionary present
and the future darkened
the smelling drunk
who showed you a parking space
the very one who sleeps
on the pavement
friend to lice

in memory of
those who make endless lines
at the Salvation Army
that miserable motherless thug
who snatched my purse
only to be stopped dead in his tracks
by the rambling of a nine millimetre
the beautiful and naive rural girl
who came to the city

and now sells her body to you
for the bread she eats
and the make-up she wears

in memory of
you whose three-month old baby
was suffocated to death in bed
by a teargas canister
one who embraces the emptiness
because those you know
are swallowed by the unknown
you who is haunted by
visions you prefer wiping out

in memory of
all who live in perpetual fear
of the unknown enemy
the enemy inside
men women
and children alike
in memory of their broken spirits

in memory of
your anguish and death
we bear the scars
in memory of
your joys
beauty and existence
we celebrate life

31 *the maximum prison in Tshwane (Pretoria) where political
    activists were held and sentenced to death by the rope*

Freedom Square

what is this buzz I hear
the heavy stampede of boots
roaring like the tumult of the sea
bursting like the volcano
rattling my tenth-floor window panes
and swaying my flat like a reed

freedom square
where you are awakened
by a freedom song
and the rhythm of *toyi-toyi*[32]
our movement's shirts
in their red and yellow
reminders of the struggles to be waged
in these days of negotiations
they capture the past
they display the suffering of workers
they revitalise mass action
that was once our pillar
but is now seemingly forgotten
except to be only re-called
when the negotiators stall

freedom square
where we wave
our flags

ANC the Party COSATU
the Mass Democratic Movement
here you can feel
you can say
the people shall govern

32 a morale boosting chant and dance by comrades

Visions of war

lanky shadows
bodies staggering in the dark
swallowed by engulfing flames
artillery-men charging upon
the throng of song and cry
of youth
that is stumbling
as it dashes for life

Senzangakhona's[33] hills

collapsed mud houses
sun-baked red soil
charred kraals
scattered belongings
of a hurried departure
a lonely restless
rifled walkie-talkie man
on the lookout
a nerve wrecking silence
on the hills of Senzangakhona

33 *the name of Shaka's father, used here to refer to KwaZulu-Natal*
   during the turbulent period of violence which was erroneously
   called black-on-black violence. In fact, the violence was caused
   and sponsored by the apartheid security

Ke nako[34]

my lungs have caught
the breath of fresh air
our winters of discontent
are warm
fires that scorched our village
have been put out
and the chilling voices
that sang *thula sizwe*[35]
rise from the ash heaps
to commanding heights
it is time to remake the graves
we left hurriedly
and let everyone know
that they have a right to live

34 *meaning, now is the time*
35 *refrain/chorus from a hymn, which was popular among the
    youth. It is an appeal to the nation to calm down, not cry
    against the brutalities meted out on them, because their God
    will overcome for them*

Be counted

they said I should write
I refused
they said I should speak
I was silent
because I chose privilege
not truth
now the resilient ones
have vanished
I remain with their offspring
the children
ask of them and their life
I cannot speak
because I am eternally mute
I cannot write
because the invaders
cut my arms off
now I sit and gaze
at the corpses of their children
with a painful memory
and a torrent of tears
running down my cheeks

Confessions

for aeons their memory
kept them alive
sewing and knitting
them together

but at times the liberator
tries to suppress his memory
because it has no apology
when it tells the truth
displaying even his cruelty
before his eyes
leaving him bare
to the pain he knows

yet memory is their ultimate hope
their resilience
a reflective mirror
of their distasteful past
their present ceremony
and their future desire
to reach new heights

like a never weary navigator
memory leads them on
from generation to generation
on a voyage
from whatever
to wherever-whenever
never to repeat their faults
never to seek revenge
on those who harmed them

The song, bloody sounds

sounds fill my head
as I ponder my destiny
holding on to memories
of those I left behind
and those who fell
sound transforms into a song
that comes in images
of armoured soldiers
whose thumping boots
lend an unsettling rhythm
that causes the people
to scatter for shelter
but the children rewrite
the song's lyrics
with outstretched arms
releasing fiery cocktails
and the ululation of an
AK-a-ka-ka-ka[36]
everyone rise
in a ninety degrees high dance
lifting clouds of dust
the tune of the song
then gushes forth blood red
From the swaying bodies
that are now lying stiff
in the streets
and the songs linger on
through tears on our cheeks
creating a river of hope
for the certainty
of our freedom

36 imitating the sound of the AK47 rifle

Truth (C)omission

the final report reads
with numerous blackened pages
the men
who sanctioned the killings
by the security agents
and marauding *amabutho*[37]
have a court interdict
that prevents the mention
of their names and deeds
the report is silent
on the big companies
and their financial support
for the government that killed us
the white businessmen
refused to attend the hearings
the report does not
have the details
of why the white media
told lies to everyone
the media men
just read a general apology
to gain a blanket amnesty
for the information
they continue to hide

37 *a regiment, warriors; here in reference to the Zulu men who used
to attack township residents and activists*

The Vlakplaas crematorium[38]

a metre high pile
of barbecue wood
a metre more
of flames
leaping higher
to swallow
the roasting bodies
lighting up the faces
of alcoholic chit-chat
in my dark backyard

38 *in memory of the "Cradock Four"; Goniwe, Calata, Mkhonto*
   and Mhlawuli. Cradock is a small town in the Eastern Cape
   province and the four were leaders of the United Democratic
   Front (UDF), murdered by the apartheid security. The apartheid
   agent, involved in the killing, testified at the Truth and
   Reconciliation Commission (TRC) that they had braai – barbecue
   – while they were burning the bodies of the four

The General's present[39]

only ashes
like granules of sand
leaving a trail
under the blazing sun
to tell a horrendous tale
of the men
who disappeared without trace
at the Port Elizabeth airport
now only ashes remain
as a reminder
of my troubled tale

39 for the PEBCO 3 (Port Elizabeth Black Civic Organisation) and
    many others who disappeared without trace, and the apartheid
    agents later testified that they burnt their bodies and dumped
    their ashes in rivers, etc

I want to know

my quest for truth
nails me down
for death to laugh
in my face

Miscarriage[40]

the foetus yelled
from the internals
of its carrier
feeling a separation
with the umbilical chord
as the body was
flung across
the four cornered concrete
there
on the cold cement floor
a red puddle stood

40 for the many women who had miscarriages from the physical
   torture they endured while incarcerated

Partial memory loss[41]

chapter one
arrest recalled
in moving pictures
chapter two
loud screams
under electric shocks
blanked out of the mind
chapter three
life or death
lost pages
in a frightening dossier
of the sergeant's report

41 *almost all the apartheid security men claimed not to remember
what happened and what they did*

The unmarked grave[42]

hurriedly thrown bones
crushed skull
clattered like scrambled eggs
defamed and deformed
beyond recognition
fossilised excavations
of a national archaeological
expedition
buried under a soil heap
daily trudged upon
where a footpath emerges
amidst the wild shrubs

42 *for Barney Molokwane and his MK unit. They were captured
and killed after successfully blowing up Sasol. Their remains
were excavated by the TRC's Investigating Unit in November
1997 in an unmarked grave in Mpumalanga's town of Piet
Retief. And this is to many others in graves still unknown*

Grave waters[43]

ash remains of a hideous
crematorium
afloat
the silent waters
where the fisherman once
made earnings
those days
when the woman quenched
the family's thirst
from its soothing water
the time when children
refreshed their bare bodies
in its deepest ends

now
everyone is in awe
of the river
they choose to stay away
except for the relatives
who come to pay their
last respects
to those buried here
by the security henchmen

43 *for Siphiwe Mtimkhulu, a courageous student leader from Port
Elizabeth, who was poisoned, maimed and ultimately confined
to a wheelchair. He too was in the end burnt by the security men
and the remains thrown in the river, so the apartheid agents
said at the TRC*

The painter child

the child paints
in water colours
of tears streaming
down a mother's cheeks
the child draws
dots from red spots
that remain
on the chilling concrete floor
the child has few colours
mostly they are red
from the ceaseless trail
of red streams
at one time they look white
from the rising smoke of teargas
sometimes they are grey
from the human ash
at other times pitch black
from the burnt-out tyres
then the child paints profusely
mostly with red
from the veins of those
who burnt the tyres

Nene[44]

little girls chatter
as they play skipping[45]
a thunderous sound
disrupts the playfulness
in my street
one little girl falls
and the others run away
as the ground
turns red
her distraught mother runs
against the escaping children
then she sees
where her little girl stood
before the SAP[46] cleared the evidence
when they took her
lifeless body away

44 *she was between 10 and 14 years old when a soldier's bullet*
   killed her in September 1985 in 'Maletsoai (Aliwal-North). Many
   children her age died in similar fashion while playing in the
   streets
45 *a township game - mostly played by girls - that requires great*
   skill moving through the stages. The game uses women's
   leggings, cut quite thin, and one must separate them using
   one's feet
46 *South African Police - sometimes called satan after people by*
   the people

Apollo's[47] flight

amidst the qha! qha! qha![48]
of stones
the rumbling of the molotov
the whistling of the
phatlha-phatlha[49] of youth
Apollo wishes to fly
almost invisibly
bursts forth from the
shadowy interior
of the candle-lit m'khukhu[50]
and comes to rest
in his mother's arms
except
through the muzzle of his
automatic machine-gun rifle
the soldier has other thoughts
to send Apollo on a no return flight
to the great Tlatlamatjholo[51]

47 *he, like Nene, was a small boy who happened to have been in*
   the street of his township - 'Maletsoai. He ran for cover when
   the soldiers started shooting, but the bullet went through the
   corrugated iron of the shack where he was and killed him. He
   died in August 1985
48 *sound of stones, rocks*
49 *sound of running*
50 *shack*
51 *the creator, God*

The landless native[52]

he had dared to pen
the poignant questions
that had the white man's
back up
even before the
ink dried on the paper
his death was foretold
in the one-way exit permit
to the USA
maybe he missed home
too much to wait
for the white rulers
to permit his return
or maybe someone else
had the better mind
to quickly fly him from
a seventh floor apartment
and splatter his brains
on the New York streets
where he rests in Fern Cliff
a few steps away for Malcolm X

52 Nat Nakasa, journalist. Whether or not he committed suicide, his death remains a symbol of the alienation and psychological harm caused by apartheid on black people. His remains were repatriated from the New York, USA, to Chesterville, his birthplace, in KwaZulu-Natal and laid to rest on September 13th 2014

Never again

for many years I heard you
arbitrarily change my name
and disgrace my race
intent on changing my appearance
you defaced me
and my gaze with your brutality
I could feel your hatred
and my veins recoiled with rage
when you debased my home
then I could not take it any longer
I fought you back and won
to regain my dignity

Collective amnesia[53]

when memory fades
so does our existence
and with it
our collective conscience

thus
our bodies are numb
indifferent to the anguish
of their youth
our mouths dumb
against the monumental background
of outspoken peoples
our ears deaf
to the wail of skeletons
of our young

those who wish
to remember
face a tirade
of unforgiving conciliators
who trade their infants' blood
for a drunken stupor
in open air gatherings
that reduce their memory
to meaningless semi-naked gyrations
before lustful eyes

that is when
memory fades
like someone

taking away your home
and sending you
into a treacherous wilderness
without a spear
or a shield
when memory fades
so does our existence
and with it
our collective conscience

53 *a lament for the way June 16 was celebrated in the early 1990s*
   in the name of "reconciliation" and freedom

Love in war

time and space
complicate everything
I left in haste under a
cloak of secrecy
it was so that they
would not suspect you knew
when they came around
looking for me

even as I want
to be with you I cannot
so inside my green book[54]
I keep the letter you wrote me
when I was in prison
this way I can hear you
talk to me all the time

I am torn inside
I do not know how
I can stay here
and be with you
so each day I read
the note you left behind
the morning of my secret getaway
"please don't forget to buy the bread"
then in me hope springs eternal
that soon I'll return home
to your loving arms
and together
we will break bread again

54 the ANC's revolutionary political-military strategy on how to conduct the struggle in South Africa. It was developed after an ANC delegation - led by OR Tambo - visited Vietnam in 1978. The lessons resulted in what came to be known as the four pillars of struggle - mass mobilisation, armed struggle, underground work and international solidarity

Don't be silenced

my country bleeds in
silence
being mute is painted
in rainbow coloured pictures
of Tutuanism[55]
the silence is deafening
and deadly

the tiny voice inside
shoves me into a sorrowful howl
in tears that recall
the bloodshot eyes
of a fourteen year old boy
after the Special Branch[56] men
electrocuted his balls in interrogation

the voice inside me demands
that I tell of those
who despised death
so that we may live
it compels me
to raise the names
of those who fell
into the khatampi[57]

I want
to scream loud
the names of the hyenas
to whom they fell victim
and chronicle the criminal acts

178

of the covert operatives
otherwise my silence
will be a betrayal
to those who did not
make it to the
Truth and Reconciliation Commission
and like those
who can no more
speak for themselves
my silence
will be deadly

55 *in reference to the renowned Archbishop Desmond Tutu, head of*
the TRC, who liked calling South Africa a 'rainbow nation' after
1994. Quite apt when considering colours of the rainbow do not
mix and the black pot of gold is invisibly somewhere at the end/
tip of the rainbow. Unfortunately he, like many, thought it was
an appropriate resonance to our country's diversity
56 *this was a security division that had previously been operating*
as a Criminal Investigation Division (CID) but turned into a
single focus of hunting down, arresting, and interrogating
political activists.
57 *an abyss*

Dream and dare

trapped between the bullet
and the stone
when the only chance against
the grave
was to run
we dared to dream

when friends were few
hospitality a human solidarity
in lands we did not know
and homes of strangers
we dared to dream

when youth was compelled
into adulthood
water a privileged drop of
wishful thinking
when the possibility of coming
home alive
was immunity to malaria
or cleaning pigs
to avoid the impipi's[58] cell
we dared to dream

when to preserve life
was to give yours away
we dreamt
even when the dream
seemed daring
we dared to dream

58 snitch, informer

The song, music-man

the music goes on
and the child continues playing
hearing the song
through tears on the cheeks
the child refuses to dance
but the heart taps
to the rhythm
forcing the motionless torso
to sway in twitches
and trance-like movements
which picture life histories
of stories not yet said
thus
the child dances
yet no one hears the music
but the child feels it
can almost touch it
and yet
the child still refuses to sing
save through his mute tongue
and tightly closed lips
eyes shut
the song propels itself
out of him
because the song
is all over him
and everywhere in him
as such
the music goes on
and the child carries on playing

The bomb blast

pieces of flesh
fly across the burning sky
bringing the rush hour traffic
into a crushing halt
news from the state broadcaster
sends shivers into white suburbia
while the voice of the
minister of law and order
grinds out assurances
that they are in control
of the situation
against the so-called
communist terrorists
who are intent
on sowing seeds of discontent
inside their otherwise
well-mannered black population
for that moment we had power
and sometimes
when I look back
I enjoy the sky-licking flames
of Sasol

Seeing through the wounds

the aching from the wound
you caused is no more
but a gaze at the silent scar
casts us into deeper
realms of vision
that only the pain
in the heart speaks of
every scar
has a memory
and every wound
its own story
so my tears create a hope
they express
through the blood that flows

I am freedom

this freedom is mine
like the preciousness of this skin
I am freedom
I was in the streets
here and abroad
in Malange and Sign O' Rama[59]
to give birth
to the miracle of the world
I am the endless lines
in the first ballot
that perched you
in your rightful place
among peoples and nations
and draped you
in your united
but diverse colours

59 Sign O'rama was where the special branch held and tortured
    political activists in the town of 'Maletsoai. The other is a place
    in Angola

Masapo[60]

touch that stone
with care
it may be someone's tombstone
do not cut that forest carelessly
maybe the spirits live in it
walk humbly on that ground
it may be someone's grave
submerged in the open space
tread lightly
never forget
lest you crush the bones
rested where you stand
they are your making
they are who you are

60 meaning bones. The term has many meanings in the African
languages among them, ancestors, the dead. Families, of those
who were killed and went missing during the struggle for
liberation in South Africa, implored the TRC - and the new
democratic government - to help them "return the bones" of
their loved ones. The meaning being that the remains must be
found so the families can pay their final respect. For as long as
the bones are not returned, there will be no closure in the lives
of the families and our country

The future

The hashtag generation
2015 class

the next harvest is foretold
in the summer breeze
as I watch the children
make the transition
mukoma[61] the children won
the children have taken us
midway through a raging torrent
from the west
they blew past spring
and came down in a summer gush
the streets awash with their plumage
writing in red
on the doors of freed lawmakers
while wrestling with law enforcers
shamwari[62] the children won
under the blazing sun of Johannesburg
in contrast to the black power salute
in the cold winter march
to Orlando stadium
on June 16 1976
mzala the children bulldozed
past austerity
clothed in jacaranda leaves
giggling with number one[63]
before Christine Lagarde[64] rung
it is just the first hurdle
they say

next they'll gain the freedom
we desire
the freedom we fought for
#weareontherise

61 *friend, comrade*
62 *friend*
63 *a phrase one would hear when people talk about the President*
    in South Africa. In this reference it is President Jacob Zuma. The
    poem is a celebration of the university students movement for
    the transformation (decolonisation) of universities and for free
    education, #feesmustfall
64 *the World Bank/IMF boss*

Printed in the United States
By Bookmasters